Play It Again, Sam

Written by Pamela Rushby
Illustrated by Kat Chadwick

Published by Pearson Education Limited, 80 Strand, London, WC2R 0RL.

www.pearsonschools.co.uk

First published in 2010 by Pearson Australia.
This edition of *Play It Again, Sam* is published by Pearson Education Limited by arrangement with Pearson Australia. All rights reserved.

Text © Pearson Australia 2010
Text by Pamela Rushby

Original illustrations © Pearson Australia 2010
Illustrated by Kat Chadwick

22 21 20 19 18
10 9 8 7 6 5 4 3 2 1

British Library Cataloguing in Publication Data
A catalogue record for this book is available from the British Library

ISBN 978 0 435 19425 3

Copyright notice
All rights reserved. No part of this publication may be reproduced in any form or by any means (including photocopying or storing it in any medium by electronic means and whether or not transiently or incidentally to some other use of this publication) without the written permission of the copyright owner, except in accordance with the provisions of the Copyright, Designs and Patents Act 1988 or under the terms of a licence issued by the Copyright Licensing Agency, Barnards Inn, 86 Fetter Lane, London EC4A 1EN (www.cla.co.uk). Applications for the copyright owner's written permission should be addressed to the publisher.

Printed in China by Golden Cup

Acknowledgements
We would like to thank the following schools for their invaluable help in the development and trialling of the Bug Club resources: Bishop Road Primary School, Bristol; Blackhorse Primary School, Bristol; Hollingwood Primary School, West Yorkshire; Kingswood Parks Primary, Hull; Langdale CE Primary School, Ambleside; Pickering Infant School, Pickering; The Royal School, Wolverhampton; St Thomas More's Catholic Primary School, Hampshire; West Park Primary School, Wolverhampton.

Note from the publisher
Pearson has robust editorial processes, including answer and fact checks, to ensure the accuracy of the content in this publication, and every effort is made to ensure this publication is free of errors. We are, however, only human, and occasionally errors do occur. Pearson is not liable for any misunderstandings that arise as a result of errors in this publication, but it is our priority to ensure that the content is accurate. If you spot an error, please do contact us at resourcescorrections@pearson.com so we can make sure it is corrected.

Contents

Chapter 1
The Piano Moves In 5

Chapter 2
A Special Piano 13

Chapter 3
We Make a Deal 20

Chapter 4
We Never Talked About Time 26

Chapter 5
Miss Crotchet Has an Idea 34

Chapter 1

The Piano Moves In

Great-Gran handed me a cardboard box. "Here's something else for the garage sale, Sam," she said. "Put it with all the other things, please."

"Oh, Gran," said my mum. "Are you sure? You've had that rose-patterned dinner set for years."

"I never really liked it," said Great-Gran.

I put the box next to the pile of things marked "MAKE AN OFFER". I stood up and looked around.

Play It Again, Sam

Great-Gran's garage was full of furniture and crockery and garden tools, all with neat price tags. Mum and Dad and I had been working all morning. We were helping Great-Gran to get ready for her garage sale.

Mum was looking a bit upset. "I think it's really sad," she said. "I know you won't need to take much with you to the retirement home, but won't you miss everything?"

The Piano Moves In

Great-Gran held up a green table lamp with a bright orange fringe on it. "Miss this?" she said. "You've got to be joking!" Then she saw how upset Mum really was. She gave Mum a hug. "No, dear, I won't miss these things," she said. "I'm taking everything I really want to keep. As for the rest – well, I'll be glad to get rid of it."

"Won't you miss *any* of your things once you've moved to the retirement home, Great-Gran?" I asked.

"Well, yes," said Great-Gran slowly. "I'll miss my piano. But there's just no space in my new little room." She looked upset. "I would have liked you to have it some day, Sam." Great-Gran shrugged her shoulders and smiled. "Oh well," she said. "It's only a piano, after all."

She hurried off to see if Dad had finished sorting out the garden tools.

Play It Again, Sam

Mum and I went into Great-Gran's house. Her piano was standing in the lounge.

The piano was old. It was made of dark, polished wood. It was so old that the white keys had gone a deep cream colour. I touched one of them gently. It made a soft, deep noise.

"I wonder if it would fit in our back room," Mum said, with a thoughtful look.

"No way," I said. "It's too big. We'd have to get rid of the pool table."

The Piano Moves In

Mum looked at me as if that was the best idea she'd heard all day.

"No!" I said. "We can't get rid of the pool table!"

But that weekend, Dad moved the pool table out into our garage, and the piano appeared in our back room.

Play It Again, Sam

Great-Gran was happy that we had the piano. But I didn't like it. It was so big, so dark, and somehow I felt as if it was... watching me. That was silly though. Pianos can't watch people!

The Piano Moves In

A few days later, I liked it even less.

Dad and I were on our way out to the garage to play pool. Mum was looking at the piano.

"You know," she said, "it's pretty silly having a piano in the house if no one plays it, don't you think?"

"None of *us* can play the piano," said Dad.

Play It Again Sam

"No," said Mum, "but someone could learn."

"I'm too busy," said Dad quickly.

"So am I," said Mum. Then they both looked at me.

"Hey!" I said. "Hey! I'm busy too! I've got homework and Beavers and football and the dog to take for walks …"

Mum and Dad were still looking at me.

"I'm too busy!" I cried.

But I knew it was no use.

Chapter 2
A Special Piano

My piano teacher's name was Craig.
He was a music student at the university.

I liked Craig. He had a ponytail down his back and he wore little round glasses. But I didn't like the lessons. Craig came to our house each week. He gave me a lesson. He left exercises for me to practise. It wasn't really a lot of work. But there was a big problem.

Play It Again Sam

The problem was me. I was just no good at playing the piano. As soon as I started to play, my fingers felt thick and slow and clumsy.

I really did try. I didn't want to disappoint Mum and Dad and Great-Gran. So I practised every day. It took me ages to learn the exercises properly, and the practising took up all my spare time. Now there was hardly any time to play football, or take my dog for walks.

It only took a couple of lessons for Craig to realise I wasn't much good. "Did you practise at all this week, Sam?" he asked me.

"Yes, I really did," I said. "I know it sounds awful – but I *did* practise!"

A Special Piano

Craig thought for a moment. "Sam," he said kindly, "some instruments just don't suit some people. Maybe the piano's not your thing. Have you thought about maybe the violin – or the flute – or the drums?"

That was a new idea. "Drums!" I said. "Wow! I'd love to play the drums! But I can't," I said to Craig.

I told Craig about Great-Gran and her piano.

"Looks like you're stuck with it, Sam," said Craig. "Well, we'll do the best we can. Let's go over those exercises again."

But I didn't get much better at them.

Play It Again, Sam

The next week, I was determined to get my exercises right. I'd play that piano if it was the last thing I did!

I practised every afternoon. Out of the window, I could see the other kids playing football.

Even though I practised and practised, the exercises just wouldn't come out right. Every time I hit a wrong note, I tried again and hit the same wrong note. Again. And again.

At last, I lost my temper.

I stopped playing and thumped the piano keys as hard as I could. **"I'll never do it!"** I shouted. "I'll never play this horrible piano!"

"Hey!" said a voice. "Stop hitting me – maybe I can help you."

I stopped dead. "What?" I said. Because, believe it or not, it was the piano that had spoken to me.

A Special Piano

A piano talking to you isn't a thing that happens every day. I'd always thought this piano was a bit strange, but I certainly hadn't expected it to talk to me!

"Well, at least you've stopped thumping me," growled the piano. "Though I must say your playing isn't much better than thumping. You're not very good at playing a piano, are you?"

"No," I said. "But I do practise!"

Play It Again, Sam

The piano sighed. "I know you do," it said. "Every day. Boring little exercises. Up and down. Over and over!"

"I have to practise," I said. "I don't like it much, but I do it."

"Well … maybe you won't have to practise any more," said the piano.

"What do you mean?" I said.

"You may have noticed," said the piano, "I'm a rather special piano."

"Well, yes," I said. "You can talk."

"Not only that," said the piano. "I can play by myself."

A Special Piano

I thought about that. "So?" I said.

The piano jangled its keys. "Think about it!" it said. "If I do the playing, you won't have to! It'll look as if you're playing, but really it'll be me. You won't have to practise any more!"

Chapter 3
We Make a Deal

I liked the idea of not having to do any more piano practice! But it did make me wonder. "Why should you help me?" I asked the piano. "What's in it for you?"

"I like to be played," said the piano. "I love music. But I can't play without someone sitting on the piano stool. It would give away my secret."

We Make a Deal

"Let me get this straight," I said. "All I have to do is sit here and look as if I'm playing, and you'll do the rest?"

"That's right," said the piano happily.

It sounded good to me.

Play It Again Sam

"It's a deal," I said. "When do we start?"

"Right now," said the piano.

"Okay," I said. "Here are my exercises. Can you play them?"

I put the music onto the music stand.

The piano was silent for a moment. "Simple!" it said.

All of a sudden it played the exercises. Perfectly. My fingers, which had been resting on the keys, were pulled along as it played. It looked just as if I was playing the notes.

"Wow!" I said. My week's music practice was finished. I was free!

I started to jump off the piano stool.

"Hey! Wait a minute!" said the piano. "What about our deal?"

I stopped. "Our deal?" I said.

We Make a Deal

"Sure," said the piano. "I do your exercises, and then I get to play the music I like. Remember?"

"Oh. Yes. All right," I said.

"Come on," said the piano. "Sit down. It has to look as if someone's playing me, doesn't it?"

I sat down again. "Ready," I said.

"I'd better make them fairly easy pieces," said the piano. "So it'll sound as if you are playing them."

I thought that was probably a bit of an insult. But then I didn't have time to think any more. The piano was away. It played and it played. Waltzes and marches. Quick tunes and slow ones. Classical music and rock. My fingers were pulled all over the keyboard.

Up and down, up and down,

following the notes the piano played.

 **Play It Again Sam**

At last, the piano stopped. "Ohhh," it said. "That was great! I haven't had such a wonderful play in years!"

I stared at my fingers. I was surprised they weren't worn right off.

"Can I go now?" I said.

"Of course," said the piano. "Same time tomorrow?"

"All right," I said. I went out to play football.

We Make a Deal

I'll have to see how this goes, I thought. By the time the piano had finished playing, I didn't have much time for football. Maybe this wasn't going to be such a great deal after all.

Chapter 4
We Never Talked About Time

Every day, the piano played my exercises. Then it played for itself. Every day, it played a little bit longer than the day before.

Of course, Mum and Dad noticed how my playing was improving.

"We're so proud of you, Sam," they said. "It just shows what practice can do."

We Never Talked About Time

"Sure," I said. I was sitting at the piano. I'd been there for an hour. The piano had had a great time, but I was exhausted.

"Great-Gran's coming for afternoon tea next Sunday," Mum said. "She'll be so pleased!"

"Great," I said.

Craig was pretty pleased too.

Play It Again, Sam

"I've never seen anything like it," he said. "You weren't tricking me before, were you, Sam?"

"Not me," I said. "Maybe it just sort of ... clicked ... all of a sudden?"

Craig still looked unsure. "Well, maybe," he said. He scratched his head.

"Play it again, Sam"

So I did. Or, rather, the piano and I did.

That night, Great-Gran called.

"Great-Gran wants to know if she can bring her friend, Miss Crotchet, to tea on Sunday," said Mum.

We Never Talked About Time

"Sure," said Dad and I.

"Miss Crotchet used to be a piano teacher," said Mum. "She's really interested in Sam's playing. She'd like to hear him."

"Sure," said Dad again. "Why not?"

I wasn't so keen. Craig hadn't spotted what was going on, but maybe Miss Crotchet would. But how could she know? No one could ever know!

"Do you think you'll have learned all your new exercises by Sunday, Sam?" said Mum.

"No problem at all," I said.

Play It Again, Sam

During that week, I had lots of problems. The piano was getting worse and worse. It wanted to play on and on, every day. Waltzes and marches. Quick tunes and slow ones. Classical music and rock. It played them all.

At last, on Saturday afternoon, I got fed up. "That's it," I said. "I've been here for hours. I'm going out to play football."

"Oh, no," said the piano. "Not just yet."

"You can't stop me," I said. "I'm going right now."

"Sit down, Sam," it said. "We're not finished yet."

I backed slowly away from the piano. Suddenly, I was scared of it. "That's the end," I said. "I'm never going to play you again!"

"Oh, yes," said the piano. "I think you will."

We Never Talked About Time

I didn't like the way it said that. "You can't make me!" I said.

"I think I can," said the piano. "Don't you feel like playing … right now?"

31

Play It Again, Sam

"No!" I said. "I don't!"

Suddenly, I found myself sitting at the piano. I couldn't stop myself. My hands moved onto the keys, and the piano started to play.

"Stop it!" I shouted. "Stop it!"

"Certainly," said the piano. "Just as soon as I finish this piece." When it had finished the piece of music, it stopped. I could take my hands off the keys.

"That was horrible!" I said. "Don't ever do that again!"

"I won't have to," said the piano. "You just have to keep to our deal. I do your exercises, then I get to play what I like."

We Never Talked About Time

"But you play for too long!" I said.

"We never talked about time," said the piano.

The piano was right. We hadn't talked about time at all. It looked as if I was trapped!

Chapter 5
Miss Crotchet Has an Idea

On Sunday, Great-Gran and her friend Miss Crotchet came over for tea.

I played all my exercises for them. The piano behaved beautifully. Every piece was perfect.

Miss Crotchet Has an Idea

"That's wonderful, Sam!" said Great-Gran. "You must be very talented, dear." She turned to Miss Crotchet. "Don't you agree, Jan?"

"Oh, yes, Grace," said Miss Crotchet. "Very talented indeed."

While Great-Gran talked to Mum and Dad, Miss Crotchet came over to me. "Tell me about your piano, Sam," she said.

"It used to be Great-Gran's," I said nervously. "It's very old."

"Mmmmm," said Miss Crotchet. "I've met pianos like yours before. Once or twice. They like to get their own way, don't they?"

Play It Again, Sam

I stared at her.

Miss Crotchet smiled at me. "Do you want to tell me about it?" she said.

So I did. All of it. "I don't want to learn the piano any more!" I said, at the end. "I'd like to play drums. I hate this piano!"

"Oh, poor piano," said Miss Crotchet. "It just wants to be played, Sam, but I can see it's not being nice to you … Hmm, I've got an idea."

Great-Gran came over to me. "Sam, dear, I've been talking to your mum and dad," she said.

Miss Crotchet Has an Idea

"You're playing so well that I'd like to pay for extra piano lessons for you. Would you like that?"

Like it? I was horrified.

"Oh no!" I said.

Great-Gran blinked in surprise. "No?" she said.

Miss Crotchet put her hand on my shoulder. "I think what Sam would be really good at is playing the drums," she said.

"The drums?" Mum, Dad and Great-Gran all said.

Play It Again, Sam

"Yes, the drums," said Miss Crotchet firmly.

"But – what about the piano?" said Mum.

"Well," said Miss Crotchet, "I think we need a piano at the retirement home. In the lounge." She turned to Mum. "Quite a lot of people in the home can play the piano, you know."

She put her hand on the piano. It seemed as if she were speaking to it. "I think the piano would be played almost all the time."

Miss Crotchet Has an Idea

My hands were resting on the piano keys. Suddenly, I felt the keys move. It was as if the piano understood what Miss Crotchet was saying – and it liked the idea.

"The drums, eh?" said Mum and Dad.

"Yes. The drums," said Miss Crotchet.

So that's what happened.

The piano went off to the retirement home, and Craig teaches me the drums now. I love it.

Play It Again Sam

Next Sunday, we're going to Great-Gran's new home for tea. Maybe I'll be able to have a quick word with the piano. I have a feeling it's going to tell me it's very happy.